You Are Healed

By
Robb Thompson

You Are Healed
ISBN 1-890900-42-7
Copyright © 2000 by Robb Thompson
Family Harvest Church
18500 92nd Ave.
Tinley Park, Illinois 60477

Editorial Consultant: Cynthia Hansen
Cover Design: Bryant Design

Dedication

I dedicate this book to all those who are searching for God's healing power and to those who want to build a foundation of healthy living through the Word of God.

Table of Contents

Introduction vii

Man's Opinion or God's Word on Healing? 1

Healing Must Be *Pursued* 21

Different Ways Jesus Heals 31

Believing God for Yourself 47

Adjusting Your 'Receiver' 69

Introduction

Divine healing is one of the most elusive graces you and I have been given in this life. Why? Because the only proof we have for our healing until it is manifested is that which the Word of God says.

Nevertheless, God's Word is all the proof we need. The principles of God's Kingdom will always be greater than anything this world can ever produce for us. We just have to learn how to apply these principles to our lives until we are walking in the divine health God has always intended that we walk in.

This book is in part a fulfillment of the mandate God has given me to help believers learn to live as *winners* in Jesus Christ. I want to bring *you*, dear reader, into a deeper relationship with Christ – a vital fellowship in which you can enjoy the divine health Jesus already paid for when that whip was laid across His back.

You don't have to be dependent on the fivefold ministry for your victory in any arena of life – including healing. You can enter by your own faith into the winner's circle God has destined for you from the foundation of the earth!

By His stripes, my friend, you *were* healed. That's not man's opinion – that's reality according to Almighty God!

– Robb Thompson

Chapter 1

Man's Opinion
Or God's Word on Healing?

So many beliefs about healing are circulating both in the world and in Christendom today. People have all kinds of ideas about what God's will is or is not regarding physical healing. However, most of these doctrines of healing are manmade — developed as people try to explain *God* by looking at *man* rather than by looking at what God has said in His Word about the subject.

Later we'll look at some of man's faulty opinions on the subject of healing. But what we really need to find out first is *God's* perspective on physical healing. According to His Word, how do we get to the place where we are living a whole and healthy life?

In order to know what God thinks about *healing*, we must first understand what He thinks about *sickness*. We can learn a lot about that by going back to the beginning — to the Garden of Eden. There was no sickness in that

Garden. In fact, throughout the account of everything God created in the first two chapters of Genesis, not one mention is made of God creating any form of sickness.

Where Did Sickness Come From?

So where did sickness come from? Sickness actually came when Adam took his eyes off God and began to live his life through mere experience. In other words, *Adam began to live his life through the eyes of man rather than living it through his belief in what God said.*

You see, Romans 5:12 says, *"...through one man sin entered the world, and death through sin, and thus death spread to all men, because all sinned."* The death sentence came upon every man at the time Adam transgressed. Satan convinced Adam that God was unnecessary and that Adam could be his own god and thus disobey. But when Adam swallowed that lie and disobeyed God, he opened the door to sin.

In Deuteronomy 28:15-68, we see that sin can be divided into three parts: *sin, sickness,* and *disappointment,* which includes *poverty and lack.* In other words, the curse of sin includes the suffering that comes from continually observing with one's eyes the good things of life, yet only experiencing one horrible disappointment after another in one's own life.

God had made Adam His steward in the Garden of Eden. Adam had everything a man could ever desire in his life. Nevertheless, he believed Satan's deception and subsequently opened the door to sin, sickness, and disappointment. Thus, through Adam's deliberate, disobedient act, sickness came into the world.

Satan's Deceptive Tactics

Now, this whole process actually began when Lucifer came on the scene in the form of a serpent and said to the woman, *"...Has God indeed said, 'You shall not eat of every tree of the garden'?"* (Gen. 3:1).

Eve responded to the serpent, *"...We may eat the fruit of the trees of the garden; but of the fruit of the tree which is in the midst of the garden, God has said, 'You shall not eat it, nor shall you touch it, lest you die'"* (Gen. 3:2,3).

Then the serpent sprang his trap, pressuring her from the inside with a thought and from the outside with his evil presence. He said in effect, "Now wait a minute, Eve. I'll tell you why God said what He said. God knew that in the day you eat of that fruit, you'd be like Him, knowing good and evil" (v. 5).

The devil still uses the same old tactics today. He'll whisper to your mind, *You're getting the flu. You're getting the flu. You're getting the flu. You're getting the flu.* Then the next thing you know, you're telling someone, "I think I'm coming down with the flu." It isn't long before the devil's word to you is confirmed with signs following — you come down with the flu! You yielded to his pressure and accepted his package of sickness and lies!

So there Adam and Eve stood in the midst of the Garden. Eve was now reasoning in her mind that the tree was good for food and to be desired in order to make one wise. The Bible says that when she took of the fruit and ate it, her husband Adam was standing nearby (v. 6). He saw that nothing seemed to happen to Eve when she took a bite of the fruit.

Maybe Adam thought, *Wait a second. That tree is good for food. That's a tree to be desired to make one wise. And nothing happened to Eve when she ate some of its fruit!*

Then basing his decision on Eve's experience, Adam chose to disregard what God had said. He took of the forbidden fruit and ate it himself, thereby opening the door for sin, sickness, and disappointment to enter into the experience of the human race on this earth!

Adam's Sin
Reproduced in Us

How many times have we made the same mistake Adam did? For instance, we may have stood in faith for someone to be healed who *didn't* get healed. When we saw that nothing seemed to happen in that person's body, we quit believing that God wants to heal everyone. We quit telling people that Jesus heals. We started saying things like, "Well, you know, sometimes God heals and sometimes He doesn't. That's just the way He is." Soon we stopped telling people that God could do *anything* for them.

Why did we back off from healing? Because we allowed ourselves to live according to the disappointments of other people's experience. We began to base our theology about healing on what we saw — not on what God has said. We began to think, *Well, it looked to me like this person did everything right, and he didn't receive his healing. So why should I believe for healing for myself?*

Now, you may not come out and actually say you're not going to stand for your healing. But you begin to back away. The devil helps the process by whispering to your mind, *Has God really said that Jesus took your infirmities and bore your sicknesses? Has God really said that the same Spirit who raised Jesus from the dead lives in you? Well, then, why don't you ever experience it?*

Fear begins to dominate your life because you feel unprotected. You decide you're just going to have to try to get healed by yourself. But when you try to take care of yourself, you actually begin to hurt yourself even more.

The Folly of Focusing On Our Differences

As soon as Adam and Eve ate of the forbidden fruit, their eyes were opened, and they knew they were naked. But wait a minute. Hadn't Adam and Eve been naked the whole time? Why did they only recognize that fact after they disobeyed God? Because they didn't have God's glory clothing them any longer. Now their focus was different. Now they were focusing on *what was different* about each other rather than *what was the same*.

This is one of the greatest challenges that faces the Church of Jesus Christ today. The devil has Christians focusing on the differences among themselves rather than what makes them the same. Believers are going around saying to each other, "Listen, we have problems between us," when they should be focusing on the very thing that brings them together — their belief in Jesus Christ!

The Bible says, *"Do not be overcome by evil, but overcome evil with good"* (Rom. 12:21). Since we know that to be true, what right do we ever have to talk about our differences? Didn't Jesus pay the price for our differences?

You might say to me, "You just don't want to face the issues." No, I'm facing *the* issue. The issue is that I cannot lay anything to your charge because of what Jesus has already done for you and for me. The issue is that if I love Jesus, I have the *privilege* of loving you!

The same is true in the area of healing. As long as the devil can keep believers fighting about their different opinions and doctrines on healing, they'll never deal with the real issue, which is *why exactly are they staying sick*?

It's like a student who blames his bad grades on his teachers. "It's the instructor's fault. He doesn't know how to teach!" he says. Then one day at home, the student gets the revelation that he really needs to get good grades if he wants to pursue his chosen career. From that moment on, his grades take a 180-degree turn!

So you say to the student, "Hey, I thought the *instructor* was keeping you from getting good grades."

"Oh, it wasn't really the instructor."

No, it wasn't the instructor's fault. It never was. The reason why that student's grades were bad was his own lack of effort. He was the problem — no one else.

Blameshifting and finger-pointing is one of the devil's favorite tactics. He likes to stoke the fire of strife among those of us in the Body of Christ by getting us to blame each other for our problems and the lack of victory in our lives. Satan just keeps putting one log on the fire after another by whispering lies to our minds. And if we listen to those lies, we end up so angry at each other that we never deal with the enemy — the real source of sickness and every other problem!

Why Did Jesus Heal?

When Jesus walked this earth, He knew very well who the source of sickness and disease was. That's why He spent so much of His time ministering to those who came to Him for healing.

Remember, Jesus was all man and all God at the same time. He came from both the womb of Mary and the sperm of Heaven. So by looking at Jesus, we can begin to see a picture of who God the Father really is and what He really thinks about healing.

Jesus painted a picture of God. In John 14:9, Jesus said to Philip, *"...Have I been with you so long, and yet you have not known Me, Philip? He who has seen Me has seen the Father...."* Then in John 5:30, Jesus stressed that He didn't come to do His own will, but the will of Him who sent Him.

Jesus desired only to finish the Father's work. The greatest thing Jesus could ever be was transparent. This is why He so clearly represented the Father.

Now let's consider the picture Jesus painted of the Father's will in regard to healing. We can find two basic reasons in the Scriptures that Jesus healed people. Number one, He healed because of *His compassion.* Matthew 14:14 (*KJV*) says, *"And Jesus went forth, and saw a great multitude, and was moved with compassion toward them, and he healed their sick."*

Number two, Jesus healed because of His hatred for the works of the devil. First John 3:8 says, *"...For this purpose the Son of God was manifested, that He might destroy the works of the devil."* Also, in reference to Jesus, Hebrews 1:9 says, *"You have loved righteousness and hated lawlessness; therefore God, Your God, has anointed You with the oil of gladness more than Your companions."*

Luke 4:18 describes how Jesus went about destroying the works of the devil according to the Father's will: *"The Spirit of the Lord is upon Me, because He has anointed Me to preach the gospel to the poor; He has sent Me to heal the brokenhearted, to proclaim liberty to the captives and recovery of sight to the blind, to set at liberty those who are oppressed."*

Through everything Jesus accomplished during His earthly ministry, we can see that He despised what Satan had done to the human race, the crown of His Father's creation. Jesus saw firsthand the devastation of a world filled with people who were convinced that God was not for them but against them. With everything in Him, Jesus despised what Satan had done to God's creation. So Jesus came to reverse the curse and destroy the works of the devil!

Make the Bible
Your Basis of Doctrine

We've looked at what God thinks about healing. When you're in pursuit of healing for your body, that's all that really matters.

You know, it really is very simple. If you see it in the Bible, you do it. If you don't see it in the Bible, you don't do it. "Yeah, but that doesn't go along with our church doctrine or our tenets of the faith." Then adjust your church doctrine and redo your tenets!

First, go to the Book; *then* make the tenets. Don't figure out your church doctrine and then try to explain the Book in a way that fits your doctrine! Remember, the Bible is a recording of *God's* tenets of faith, so make it your basis of doctrine on every subject, including healing!

With that in mind, let's look at some of the faulty doctrines or beliefs about healing that are prevalent in the Body of Christ today.

*'GOD TEACHES ME
THROUGH SICKNESS'*

First, there is the belief that "God wants me sick because He is trying to teach me something." This is a particularly dangerous teaching in the Church because it keeps people in a weakened state, focusing more on what the sickness or physical hardship is supposed to teach them than on receiving the healing God has for them.

But in John 14:26, the Bible tells us that the *Holy Spirit* is our Teacher. He is to lead us into all truth (John 16:13).

People who adhere to this incorrect doctrine that sickness is sent to teach them something cite Psalm 119:67,71 as their scriptural foundation: *"Before I was afflicted I went astray, but now I keep Your word.... It is good for me that I have been afflicted, that I may learn Your statutes."* Certainly, people do learn things from the physical trials they go through. But that doesn't mean God sent the sickness into their lives to be their teacher!

If that were true, the Holy Spirit whom God *has* sent to us to be our Teacher and Guide would become unnecessary. He would be displaced by sickness or adverse circumstances as the instructor for our lives.

When I talk to people who hold to this particular doctrine, I ask them, "Have you been to a doctor?"

"Well, yes."

"Are you on medication?"

They usually respond, "Yes, I'm on medication."

Then I ask them, "So why do you want to work against God by not learning as much as you can from your sickness? If you go to the doctor and take medication, you are really trying to stop the process through which God wants to teach you."

You see, people really don't believe this doctrine that God sends sickness upon them to teach them something. Besides, if it were true, the Church would be full to the brim with very, very wise people! There wouldn't be a dummy in the Body of Christ today if people truly learned what they needed to know from sickness!

I'll tell you what *I* learned from sickness. I learned that I never want to be sick again! I learned that sickness doesn't add to a person's life; it takes away from it. I learned that you can have all the money in the world you could ever want; but if you're sick, you're poor.

Those are the lessons I've learned from sickness. I guarantee you, I'd much rather learn my lessons in life from the Teacher sent to me by my Heavenly Father — the Holy Ghost!

'GOD WANTS ME HEALED — BUT NOT RIGHT NOW'

Another faulty belief that people often hold about healing is "God wants to heal me, but He doesn't want to do it right now." In Mark 11:24, Jesus said, *"Therefore I say to you, whatever things you ask when you pray, believe that you receive them, and you will have them."* Jesus is telling us that we are to actually believe that we have something *before* we ever see it!

Hebrews 11:1 says, *"Now faith is the substance of things hoped for...."* So you first hope to be healed; then you set your faith on God's promise that you *are* healed — not that you're *going to get* healed. You see, when you talk about getting healed, you're always talking about some point in time in the future. You're putting off into the future what God has already given you in the *now*.

Never forget — "wanna-be's" in life live in the future. "Has-beens" live in the past. Successful, productive people live in the *now*!

God doesn't live in yesterday, and He doesn't live in tomorrow. He lives in your *now*. That's why He said, *"NOW faith is the substance of things hoped for...."* Your healing isn't something for tomorrow; it isn't something for yesterday. It's something for *right now*.

The woman with the issue of blood said, *"...If only I may touch His clothes, I shall be made well"* (Mark 5:28). In this woman's "now," she touched His garment and was made whole that very moment!

One day as the apostle Paul preached, he perceived that a crippled man who was listening to him had faith to be healed (Acts 14:8-10). So Paul told the man to stand up on his feet, and the man leapt up and began walking. Paul perceived that faith was present. In other words, the man had faith for *now*, not faith that maybe someday he would be healed.

When blind Bartimaeus cried out, *"...Jesus, Son of David, have mercy on me!"* all the religious people told him to be quiet (Mark 10:47,48). Even the disciples told him, "Be quiet! Don't cry out for Him!"

But the Bible says that Bartimaeus cried out all the more. Jesus stopped as a result of his "crying out all the more" and called for him to come. It wasn't a cry from Bartimaeus' mouth that caught Jesus' attention. It was the faith of his *heart*.

Bartimaeus jumped up and threw off his beggar's coat
— a sure sign that he knew he was about to be healed.
At that moment, *he gave up his yesterdays so he could
embrace God's tomorrow.*

You see, the coat designated Bartimaeus as a legal-
ized beggar. He was truly blind. He was not scamming
society. So when he threw off the coat, he threw off his
identity as a blind man and in faith walked over to Jesus,
expecting to be healed.

Jesus asked Bartimaeus, *"…What do you want Me to
do for you?…"*

The blind man replied, *"…Rabboni, that I may receive my sight"* (v. 51). Bartimaeus had faith for his healing in the now — and he instantly received his sight!

Jesus told the Canaanite woman who came to receive
healing for her daughter, *"It is not good to take the
children's bread and throw it to the little dogs."* The
woman replied, *"…Yes, Lord, yet even the little dogs eat
the crumbs which fall from their masters' table"* (Matt.
15:25-27).

That was the Canaanite woman's faith speaking for
her particular "now." She believed that her daughter
would be healed *right then* — not the next day or the
next week — and that's exactly what happened!

'IT ISN'T GOD'S WILL
TO HEAL EVERYONE'

Another unscriptural doctrine many Christians believe is "It is not God's will for everyone to be healed."

Sometimes it's His will to heal someone, and sometimes it isn't.

These believers point to Jesus' prayer in the Garden of Gethsemane where He prayed, *"...O My Father, if it is possible, let this cup pass from Me; nevertheless, not as I will, but as You will"* (Matt. 26:39). They say, "You see, even though Jesus wanted a particular thing, He didn't get it because it wasn't God's will."

But have you ever noticed that the person who says God doesn't want to heal everyone is never the one who gets healed? This person is continually looking at what is wrong with his body instead of what is right with God. Therefore, he loses sight of the fact that God considers him valuable and precious — so much so that He was willing to send His Son to die for that person's sins and to bear all his sickness and pain!

'I'm Not Worthy To Be Healed'

This leads to another reason why people do not receive healing — their sense of unworthiness. So many Christians lack an understanding of their rightstanding with God. They believe they will only be healed when they become good enough. They don't know that God has already declared them righteous, not because of their own actions but because of their faith in Him.

I learned something about this erroneous way of thinking one day while I was sitting in a chair experiencing tremendous bouts of painful symptoms in my body. It felt like I might be having a heart attack. As I sat there, I started wondering what I was doing wrong — what I had to fix in my life so I could be healed.

But suddenly I realized the problem with that way of thinking. I am God's child. God *wants* to heal me! I don't have to strive to become good enough before He will bestow His blessing of healing on me. I don't have to try to figure out everything that's wrong with me and fix up my life before I can receive my healing.

Matthew 15:31 tells us that when the people saw the miracles Jesus performed, they glorified the God of Israel. That day I recognized that over the years, I had seen many unsaved people get healed during healing meetings. So why couldn't God be glorified through *my* healing as a child of God?

I realized that even if something negative was going on in my life, I could still believe God for healing and then allow the Holy Spirit to deal with me later about making needed changes. Second Timothy 2:13 says that even when we believe not, yet God abides faithful!

Now, of course, it *is* possible for people to put up roadblocks to their healing that have to be dealt with. For instance, when people refuse to walk in love and forgiveness with others, they can actually block God's healing power from working in their lives.

Jonah 2:8 (*KJV*) says, *"They that observe lying vanities forsake their own mercy."* People often feed on their unforgiveness, focusing their energy and attention on what someone has done to them and allowing bitterness to grow within them. Until these people make the decision to forgive and then begin to walk in love, they are forsaking the mercy of healing God has given them.

Nevertheless, this fact holds true: The Heavenly Father's healing mercies are available to us as His children because of the blood of Jesus — not because of how much we've done to fix up our lives. We don't have to "get good enough" to receive our healing — we are already the righteousness of God in Christ!

Escaping Our 'Determinisms' Through God's Word

All the erroneous doctrines on healing mentioned above originate in what I call faulty "determinisms." We all live by three basic determinisms to some extent: 1) psychological, 2) physical or genetic, and 3) environmental.

Your genetic determinism dictates whether or not you look like your mom, dad, or someone else in your lineage. Your psychological determinism is made up partially by your genetics, but it is primarily comprised of the information you take in from the external world. This then mixes with your third determinism, which is environmental.

The environmental determinism is determined by where you live and the people you hang around with. These people with whom you closely associate are like the buttons on an elevator: they either take you up or they take you down in life.

A loose definition of the word "determinism" is *that from which there is no escape*. Because of the strength of the environmental determinism, you can find Full Gospel people in certain geographical areas who strongly hold particular doctrines that aren't scriptural. Why? Because they are caught in the determinism of their particular religious environment.

This is why so many Pentecostals are impoverished. They are taught about prosperity. They talk about how God wants them to prosper. But at the same time, they never act on that principle. Why? Because many of them also learned when they were younger that any increase they ever receive must always be put back into the Gospel rather than laid up as an inheritance for their children's children. Or they learned that Jesus was poor when He walked this earth. That eliminates the possibility of a good Christian being able to prosper because he would never want to be better than Jesus!

The only way to escape these faulty doctrinal determinisms is the one I already stated: Make the Bible, and *only* the Bible, your basis of belief. If you see it in the Bible, *do it*. If you don't see it in the Bible, reject it as someone else's mistaken opinion. In every arena of life, no matter what anyone else tries to tell you, *stick with what God has already said in His Word*!

Two Ditches To Avoid

Two different churches in the New Testament show us the kinds of mistakes Christians can make along this line. Regarding the gifts of the Spirit, the Corinthian church had gotten into the ditch of "Anything goes." The church was completely out of order, with no semblance of authority or discernment of right and wrong order in the operation of the gifts.

The Thessalonian church knew that Paul was having this problem with those carnal Corinthian Christians. So it's very likely that the Thessalonian believers reacted to the Corinthian church's excesses by freezing out the gifts of the Spirit in their own church. They said, "We don't want anyone prophesying or speaking in tongues. We aren't going to have any of that funny stuff."

That's why Paul had to exhort the Thessalonians: *"Quench not the Spirit. Despise not prophesyings"* (1 Thess. 5:19,20 *KJV*). They were unwilling to let the gifts operate in their midst because they couldn't keep them in the order they felt was necessary.

People do the very same thing in the arena of healing. Some Christians have all sorts of funny doctrines about healing. They attribute healing to God no matter how a person got healed. "Oh, look at how God did that. Isn't that wonderful?" With these Christians, anything goes — even unbiblical methods of healing.

On the other hand, many believers are like the Thessalonians. When certain methods of healing don't fit their doctrinal mold of how healing should come, they freeze out those methods. They want healing in their church, but only through the avenue that fits the narrow confines of their church doctrine.

You have to make sure you don't end up in one ditch or the other. Stay in the center of the road, always listening to the Word of God and to the Holy Spirit to find out what avenue He may want to use to bring about healing in each situation.

Paul's exhortation to the Thessalonians to "quench not the Spirit" applies to you as well. Don't let the Bible be just a dead book to you. Hebrews 4:12 says, *"For the word of God is living and powerful...."*

Stop holding yourself back from the Holy Spirit. Stop making your Christianity merely academic and begin to pursue Jesus as One who is *alive*. If everything inside the Book is dead to you, what makes you any different from a secular or a religious humanist?

One of the greatest mistakes Christians make in the arena of healing is to live with the Bible as a mere book while at the same time failing to live with the Holy Spirit as a Person. These believers never get out of their academics — what they *think* God said about healing — in order to allow the Holy Spirit to work healing in their bodies in whatever way He desires.

Too many people in the Body of Christ live with an "all or nothing" attitude. To these people, it's "this way or no way," "my way or the highway."

But the Holy Spirit isn't like that. He wants you well, and He has more than one way to bring your healing to pass. In fact, there are at least seven different avenues of healing revealed in the Scriptures. (We'll look at these avenues in the following chapters.) If you aren't willing to accept all the different ways the Holy Spirit could be leading you to greater health, you stand in danger of forsaking your own mercy (Jonah 2:8).

So spend some time with God and let Him talk to you about this issue of healing. Deal with the question of whether or not you've backed away from healing in your own life. Have you become an academic believer who no longer pursues healing? Have you held on to unscriptural beliefs about the subject, declaring, "That's the way I was taught in my church"? If so, get ready to make some changes!

And remember — the most important change you can make is to learn to walk with the Holy Spirit as a Person. He has been assigned by God to lead and direct you every moment of the day.

Don't live a life in which the Bible is just an academic, dead book and thus miss out on God's plan of freedom and good health for you. The Holy Spirit wants to bring you into an intimate relationship with Him. Then He can lead you into the healing and divine health that is rightfully yours through Christ!

Chapter 2

Healing Must Be *Pursued*

We have seen that Jesus was manifested on this earth to destroy the works of the devil — which certainly includes sickness and disease. But if that's why Jesus came to earth, what's the problem? Why are so many Christians still sick and defeated?

The problem filters down to us. You see, the devil works so hard at getting us not to receive God's blessings. He tries to make us question God's healing promises and wonder if they're really true. Or he tries to make us settle for just hearing about God's promises and never experiencing them.

That reminds me of the night I went to Denny's restaurant and settled for a lot less than I had expected to receive. I visit Denny's a lot because it's the only restaurant that's open at two o'clock in the morning in our part of town. One of my favorite items on the menu is a sandwich called the Superbird. This Superbird is composed of ham, turkey, tomatoes, and melted cheese on sourdough bread, and it's grilled like a grilled cheese sand-wich. It's absolutely a kicker! It makes you think, *How did something so gorgeous ever get on the menu at Denny's?*

Anyway, that night I was ready to chow down! I hadn't eaten all day, so I ordered the Superbird and then waited for it with great anticipation. I looked at the pic-ture of the sandwich in the menu and thought smugly to myself, *Self, you've got yourself a Superbird on the way! It's just about here!*

Then the waitress came and laid this sorry substitute for a Superbird in front of me. I looked at my plate in dismay and thought, *This is like trying to hold a conver-sation with a cadaver!* I mean, this thing looked beyond dead! Number one, the sandwich didn't have all the in-gredients it was supposed to have. Number two, the cheese on it wasn't melted. Number three, it wasn't grilled bread; it was toast!

To top it off, the french fries on the plate next to the sandwich looked like they had been fried three weeks ago. The Thousand Island dressing for my salad looked like pink water as it poured out. And my Coca-Cola tasted flat! I'm telling you, everything that could have gone wrong with my order did go wrong that night.

But you know what? I ate it all! That meal was worse than horrible, but I ate it anyway. I settled for what I got instead of asking for what was actually described in the menu.

That's the way many believers live their lives. They like to read the Book because it has a lot of good things to say about abundant life, but they settle for a far lower level of living. They end up trying to mold the Book around their own sorry lives. In other words, they look for scriptures to justify the lack of victory in their lives instead of saying, "Hey, life! You've got some changing to do!"

How To Pursue Healing

That's why healing must be *pursued*. The truth is, you will never experience what you are unwilling to pursue. You will never enjoy what you are unwilling to go after. You will never value what you are unwilling to chase. Healing will not come to you just because you are a Christian or because you think it is owed to you. *Healing will only come to you when you make room for it by diligently pursuing it.*

You see, you actually create a spiritual vacuum as you begin to pursue the healing power of God. Your intense desire for divine healing draws on God's power both from without and from within you, eventually effecting a change in your body. Therefore, *pursuit* is the first step to *experience*.

How do you pursue healing? Through the avenue of good teaching tapes and books and, most of all, through God's Word. Listen to and read material that fortifies in your heart God's will to heal your body. Stay away from anything that would diminish His authority and credibility in the arena of healing.

Jesus warned in Mark 4:24, *"...Take heed what you hear...."* He had good reason for saying that. If you continually listen to your body telling you, "You're not going to be healed," then you will not be healed. But if you read and continually meditate on the fact that Jesus took your infirmities and bore your sicknesses (Matt. 8:17), that truth will begin to become more real to you than the symptoms of sickness in your body.

Romans 8:11 is another good scripture to meditate on as you pursue healing: *"But if the Spirit of Him who raised Jesus from the dead dwells in you, He who raised Christ from the dead will also give life to your mortal bodies through His Spirit who dwells in you."* Plant that scripture in your heart and then speak it continually to yourself: "The Holy Spirit quickens my body and gives me new strength and vitality!"

Speak To Your Mountain

I believe one of the major reasons Christians don't receive their healing is that they *listen* rather than *speak* to themselves. They constantly listen to their own doubt-filled thoughts: *You're not going to get healed. You've been believing and confessing the Word, but it isn't working. You've been anointed with oil. Famous healing preachers have laid their hands on you. But you never really got anything — and you never will get anything because you're unworthy!*

If you spend your time *listening* to yourself, you will never hear one thing about success. But if you spend your time *speaking* to yourself according to God's promises, you will never hear one thing about failure!

You see, the devil will do his best to send all kinds of people across your path who never seem to get healed. He wants to paint a picture of defeat inside you that you can stare at and meditate on. That way, even if you're confessing with your mouth that you believe you're healed, you'll have the power of doubt and unbelief working on the inside of you to keep you from receiving your answer.

It's true — you can actually say the right words with your mouth but live according to wrong beliefs in your heart. Proverbs 23:7 says, *"For as he thinks in his heart, so is he...."* Jesus also said that you are going to have to give an account in the Day of Judgment for every evil thing you have spoken: *"For by your words you will be justified, and by your words you will be condemned"* (Matt. 12:37). This principle won't just come into operation on that great Day; it operates every day of your life as you live out the fruit of your own words!

So while you're pursuing healing, don't listen to your own thoughts of doubt. Don't listen to your pain or to other unbelieving people around you. Instead, speak to your mountain of sickness or disease. The mountain needs to hear *your* voice, not someone else's voice!

In Mark 11:23, Jesus said, *"For assuredly, I say to you, whoever says to this mountain, 'Be removed and be cast into the sea,' and does not doubt in his heart, but believes that those things he says will be done, he will have whatever he says."* Notice that Jesus didn't say we are to speak to *a* mountain. He calls it *this* mountain. In other words, we are speaking to a specific problem or obstacle in our lives.

Also, notice that we are not talking to God *about* our mountain. We are not talking to ourselves about our mountain. We are not even talking to the devil about our mountain! We are talking *to* the mountain.

Most believers spend a lot of time talking to God about the mountain in their lives. They'll walk all around it and give God a whole variety of views of the mountain. But the truth is, God already knows all about the mountain. He doesn't want to hear about it; He wants His children to say to it, "Be removed and be cast into the sea!"

What does it mean for your mountain of sickness to be removed? It means you are not going to be partially healed. You have determined that you will keep speaking to your mountain of sickness by faith until it is totally gone! Remember — it's a mountain. It took some time to become a mountain in your life; it may also take some time to leave. So don't stop speaking to it until it is completely removed and cast into the sea!

Your Tallest Mountains
Are Already Behind You

Did you know that the tallest mountains on this earth are in the sea? We can't even see them! Those mountains are greater than the Rocky Mountains or the magnificent mountains of Turkey and Tibet, yet they are hidden from our view.

The same is true for the mountains in *your* life. The biggest mountains of your life are already in the sea! You have already overcome bigger things than you will ever have to overcome in the future.

The devil wants to make you think you're growing weaker and weaker in your spiritual walk. But once you realize that you have come further in the past than the distance you still have to go, the revelation finally hits you: No matter how big your mountain of sickness looks, you can speak to it and say: "Be removed and be cast in the sea!" And if you believe in your heart what you say with your mouth, that mountain will eventually be cast behind you, never to be seen again!

So as you begin to speak to your mountain of sickness or disease, remember all the mountains of problems and obstacles that are already behind you, cast into the sea. At the time, those mountains were huge, but you don't see them anymore. You've already spoken to them and cast them into the sea. In other words; you've overcome them by your faith and obedience to God's Word. And the day will soon come when you don't see this present mountain anymore either — as you speak to it by faith, *not doubting in your heart*!

What You *Do* Tells the Story

As I said, the reason people don't get healed is that they don't pursue it. They don't value the blessings of God enough to do whatever it takes to obtain them. They find no value beyond themselves and end up pursuing only their own carnal comforts and desires.

But when you don't find value beyond yourself, my friend, you end up living a life that's absolutely disappointing. In order to enjoy divine health, you have to live your life before God consistently. That means giving yourself a "check-up from the neck up" every few days to make sure you're living your life based on what you're actually doing right according to God's Word — not what you *think* you're doing right.

You see, most of us don't act on what we say that we believe. That means we really don't believe it, because *we believe what we actually do*.

Always be more interested in what you do than in what you think. Acting on God's Word in the area of healing is the seed that will grow into a harvest of health for your body.

Is your life all tied up with doubts or wrong beliefs about healing that keep you from acting in faith on the Word? Then take the scissors of the Holy Ghost and cut those hindering ties! Get some movement in your life! Go pick on the devil for a while. Tell him to take his sickness and get away from your body in the Name of Jesus!

Whatever it takes, *pursue healing*. Seek God diligently. Speak to your mountain of sickness or disease according to His Word. Find out all you can about His avenues of healing, and then do what He tells you to do. God will honor your diligence by turning your *pursuit* into *experience* as your mountain of sickness is removed and "cast into the sea"!

Chapter 3

Different Ways Jesus Heals

The Gospels describe at least seven different ways that Jesus healed people. Every one of those ways are available to you, as well as for every other child of God. Let's look at each of these avenues of healing so we can better understand the various ways healing is obtained in people's lives.

First, the most important thing you need to know is that God *wants* you to be healed and blessed. He said in Third John 2 (*KJV*), *"Beloved, I wish ABOVE ALL THINGS that thou mayest prosper and be in health, even as thy soul prospereth."*

Don't believe anyone who tells you that it isn't God's will for you to prosper in every area of life. Prosperity is the signature of God, my friend. Anything God touches is blessed. Anything the devil touches is cursed.

Many Christians are confused over this issue because they focus in on such worldly scenes as Hollywood, Las

Vegas, and Wall Street. They see a lot of people blessed who aren't serving God; meanwhile, they *are* serving God, and they're *not* blessed. So instead of finding out what God says in His Word about prosperity, these Christians exchange the truth of God for the lie that it is more spiritual to be poor and sick.

The truth of the matter is that God wants you to prosper in the area of physical health just as He wants you to prosper spiritually, materially, and in every other way. So let's examine this scriptural principle by looking at seven different ways God heals people.

The Laying On of Hands

First, healing can come through the laying on of hands, which is one of the cardinal doctrines of the New Testament Church. Mark 16:18 says, *"...they will lay hands on the sick, and they will recover."*

We find the laying on of hands in a number of other places in the Bible as well. For instance, under the Old Covenant, the laying on of hands was a part of the priestly ritual in which the sin of God's people was atoned for through the use of the scapegoat — a type of Jesus Christ.

"Aaron shall lay both his hands on the head of the live goat, confess over it all the iniquities of the children of Israel, and all their transgressions, concerning all their sins, putting them on the head of the goat, and shall send it

away into the wilderness by the hand of a suit-
able man."

Leviticus 16:21

When the priest laid his hands on the scapegoat and
confessed the sins of God's people over it, the sins were
transferred through the priestly anointing from the people
to the scapegoat. Then the scapegoat was sent outside
the camp, bearing the iniquities of the Israelites.

In the New Testament, the Gospels give us several
instances where Jesus laid His hands on people to heal
them.

**And he could there do no mighty work, save
that he laid his hands upon a few sick folk, and
healed them.**

Mark 6:5 (*KJV*)

**When the sun was setting, all those who had
any that were sick with various diseases
brought them to Him; and He laid His hands
on every one of them and healed them.**

Luke 4:40

**But when Jesus saw her, He called her to
Him and said to her, "Woman, you are loosed
from your infirmity."**

**And He laid His hands on her, and immedi-
ately she was made straight, and glorified God.**

Luke 13:12,13

In Acts 28:8, the apostle Paul followed Jesus' example by laying his hands on a sick man, and the sick man was healed.

And it happened that the father of Publius lay sick of a fever and dysentery. Paul went in to him and prayed, and he laid his hands on him and healed him.

A person is healed through the laying on of hands when God's power is transferred from the person ministering healing to the recipient. Oral Roberts called this spiritual transfer "the law of contact and transmission."

Interestingly, the Bible doesn't tell us to say anything when we lay hands on the sick. It just tells us to lay hands on them — and then expect them to recover!

The Gifts of the Spirit

Healing can also come through the operation of the gifts of the Spirit, specifically the gifts of healing and the working of miracles. The Holy Spirit manifests these gifts through believers *as He wills* (1 Cor. 12:8-11). No one person has a particular gift of the Spirit operating through him all the time.

The gifts of healing and the working of miracles are endowments of the Holy Spirit for the specific purpose of supernaturally healing one or more individuals at a particular time. The person through whom the Holy Spirit manifests these gifts is given a special ability to receive a miracle for the individual being ministered to. But more often than not, the recipient's faith has nothing to do with it.

We can see an example of this when the gift of the working of miracles operated through Jesus at the pool of Bethesda (John 5:1-9). Jesus was on His way to a feast of the Jews in Jerusalem. But as He headed for the feast, the Holy Spirit pulled Him away from His intended path, leading Him to a specific paralyzed man lying near the pool.

Jesus asked the man if he wanted to be made whole. The man began to give religious excuses, but Jesus just told him to take up his bed and walk — and he did!

That was definitely a miracle! The man Jesus healed didn't have faith for his healing. He had his eyes set on the distant hope that an angel would stir the waters and someone would help get him in the water first. He didn't have anything going on in his heart that could have been called faith! The man was healed through the avenue of the gifts of the Spirit, manifested through Jesus.

Another instance of someone being healed through the working of miracles is found in Acts 3:1-8. Peter and John were entering the Temple at the hour of prayer when a crippled beggar called out to them for money. This man had lain there for forty years. That means he sat crippled in front of the Temple all those years when Jesus walked by, and he never had the faith to go to Jesus and get healed!

All of a sudden, Peter told the beggar to look on them. The man looked up at them, expecting to receive some money. But instead Peter told him, *"...Silver and gold have I none; but such as I have give I thee: In the name of Jesus Christ of Nazareth rise up and walk"* (Acts 3:6 *KJV*). Then Peter reached out, took the man's hand, and yanked him up — totally healed! That was a working of miracles, and it had nothing to do with that man's faith!

Both the gifts of healing and the working of miracles were in operation when Peter raised the woman named Dorcas from the dead (Acts 9:36-41). And it's very obvious in Dorcas' case that her faith didn't have a thing to do with it!

Recently in one of my meetings, a man was healed of a condition he'd had for twenty years as he listened to me preach. I never even prayed for him! And to top it off, he was a member of a denomination that doesn't even believe in divine healing!

Right in the middle of the meeting, this man took the pastor of the church where I was speaking outside and said, "Pastor, I haven't run in more than twenty years because my legs have been in such bad shape. But God just healed me! So tell you what — I'll race you around the church building!"

This man was about sixty-two years old, but suddenly he could move like a young man again! This was the gift of healing in manifestation. That man didn't know a thing about faith. All he had to do to receive was be in the audience where the Holy Spirit was moving!

The Demand of Faith

Another avenue of divine healing comes as a result of the demand of faith. In other words, God may lead us to demand in the Name of Jesus that sickness take its hands off our own or other people's bodies.

John 14:13 says, *"And whatever you ask* [demand or require] *in My name, that I will do, that the Father may be glorified in the Son."* So in regard to healing, Jesus is saying, "If you say, command, proclaim, or demand sickness to leave in my Name, I will do it. I'll take care of it." And if Jesus says He'll take care of it, He *will* take care of it!

This particular avenue of healing is often an act of faith that is done once in a particular situation by the unction of the Holy Spirit. According to James 4:7, when we submit to God's way of doing things and actively resist the devil and his works, he *will* flee from us — and take his sickness with him! Then all we have to do is continue to *stand* in the strength of the Lord and the power of His might (Eph. 6:10,13).

The Prayer of Agreement

The fourth method of healing is the prayer of agreement, which Jesus spoke of in Matthew 18:19: *"Again I say to you that if two of you agree on earth concerning anything that they ask, it will be done for them by My Father in heaven."* Tied to this verse is a scripture from the Old Testament that says one can put a thousand to flight, but two can put ten thousand to flight (Deut. 32:30).

When you enter into the prayer of agreement with another believer, you multiply your effectiveness in prayer. Ecclesiastes 4:9,10 says, *"Two are better than one, because they have a good reward for their labor. For if they fall, one will lift up his companion...."*

This scripture can be applied to the prayer of agreement. When you agree with another believer in prayer, both of you receive needed encouragement from each other to keep standing and actively applying your faith to the problem until the answer is manifested.

This is certainly true when asking God to heal another individual, which is definitely scriptural. Job 22:30 says that some *"...will be delivered by the purity of your hands."* Then in Luke 7:2-10, we read about a Roman centurion who sent Jewish elders to Jesus to ask Him to come heal his gravely ill servant. The elders urged Jesus to grant the centurion's request because he was a worthy man who prayed much and had built them a synagogue. In the end, Jesus did heal the servant according to the centurion's great faith.

So you can come together with another believer to agree in prayer for a person's healing, knowing that as you both determine to stand firm in faith on that agreement, healing *will* come to pass in that individual's life.

However, if one of the prayer partners ever quits standing in faith that the sick person will receive his healing, it ceases to be a true prayer of agreement. The minute that person breaks the agreement, he becomes a covenant-breaker, and the prayer loses its effectiveness. As Amos 3:3 says, *"Can two walk together, unless they are agreed?"*

Many times people have come to me and said, "I'd like you to agree with me about something."

"What am I agreeing with?" I ask.

"I want you to agree with me that I'm healed."

"Well, all right. I'll agree with you. You're healed in Jesus' Name."

After that, God will often bring these individuals to mind as I go through my day, and I'll say, "Father, I just want to thank You that So-and-so is healed in the Name of Jesus."

But then after a few months of standing in faith for someone, I sometimes find out that somewhere along the way, that person quit believing!

Too often this type of believer thinks, *I'll just get everyone to agree with me that I'll be healed.* The problem is, he has a "everybody's-faith-other-than-my-own" mentality, and that doesn't work.

But what do you do if you realize after entering into a prayer of agreement with someone else that you were not truly in faith at the time? You're just not sure if you or the person for whom you prayed will really be healed. In that case, you need to follow the counsel of Proverbs 6:2,3: *"You are snared by the words of your mouth; you are taken by the words of your mouth. So do this, my son, and deliver yourself; for you have come into the hand of your friend: go and humble yourself; plead with your friend."*

It is important to be honest with your prayer partner if you know that you didn't truly agree in faith when you prayed for a person's healing with him. Otherwise, he will continue to use the most precious possession he has, his time, to stand in faith for this individual's healing, unaware that you're not even in agreement with him! So if you're ever snared with the words of your mouth in this way, just be honest about it. I believe you'll be all the better for having acted honorably in the matter.

I believe that's one of the reasons God wants us to have people in our lives with whom we can agree in prayer. It keeps us honest. It keeps us standing in faith for the answer for which we have prayed.

Prayer for Another's Healing

The fifth avenue of healing ties into the last one, the prayer of agreement. This is a believer's intercessory prayer for another person.

John 16:24 says, *"Until now you have asked nothing in My name. Ask, and you will receive, that your joy may be full."* Jesus says to ask in His Name, and you will receive. This can include asking the Father for another's healing, as well as your own. The result for either prayer is the same: so that your joy may be full.

Well, if there is one thing you want full in your life, it's joy! But there is a prerequisite to having joy in your life: There must be an absence of rebellion and stupidity!

You see, many people live in disappointment most of their lives because of the decisions they've already made in the past — fleshly decisions that they knew at the time should never have been made. These people get in situations where there is so much of what I call "flesher" on them (short for "flesh pressure"), they just succumb to the devil's strategy and hope that the devil doesn't find out — as if he doesn't already know!

Learn this, my friend: *Never sow anything in your life that you don't want to reap later.* That's one big reason I don't backbite. First, I don't do it because it isn't right. Second, I don't do it because of what the Word teaches about it. Third, I don't backbite because I never want to be on the receiving end where people gossip behind *my* back.

The bottom line is this: Live your life with a clear conscience every day. Don't ever have any hidden closets in your heart. Live with no regrets. That's how you keep the channel open for God to answer your prayers and make your joy full.

Also, before you pray for another person's healing, it's a good idea to find out from him what's going on in his walk with God. Has he repented regarding with any unforgiveness or rebellion the Holy Spirit may have revealed in his life? Is there any area of his life in which he is doing what he knows God doesn't want him to do? In other words, make sure nothing is hindering God from answering your prayer for him. Then you can pray with confidence that the answer will come to pass.

Anointing the Sick With Oil

The sixth avenue of healing found in the Word is anointing the sick with oil. James 5:14 describes this method: *"Is anyone among you sick? Let him call for the elders of the church, and let them pray over him, anointing him with oil in the name of the Lord."* This same principle can be found in Psalm 133:2, where it says that brethren dwelling together in unity is as *"...the precious oil upon the head, running down on the beard, the beard of Aaron, running down on the edge of his garments."*

In many cases in the Bible, anointing oil represents the Presence of the Holy Spirit in the life of an individual. When a person was anointed with oil, it often brought soothing and healing.

You prepare a table before me in the presence of my enemies; you anoint my head with oil; my cup runs over.

Psalm 23:5

But my horn You have exalted like a wild ox; I have been anointed with fresh oil.

Psalm 92:10

Let the righteous strike me; it shall be a kindness. And let him rebuke me; it shall be as excellent oil; let my head not refuse it. For still my prayer is against the deeds of the wicked.

Psalm 141:5

And they [the disciples] **cast out many dev-
ils, and anointed with oil many that were sick,
and healed them.**

Mark 6:13 (*KJV*)

"So he [the Good Samaritan] **went to him and
bandaged his wounds, pouring on oil and wine;
and he set him on his own animal, brought him
to an inn, and took care of him."**

Luke 10:34

One of the primary uses of this avenue of healing is
to help new believers who may be having a hard time
receiving their healing. Perhaps something negative has
happened in a new believer's life. He is ashamed. He
feels he has committed an absolutely horrible sin, and
no one wants to have anything to do with him. Finally,
he calls for the elders of the church, who come and anoint
this young believer's head with oil. The Bible says that
the prayer of faith will save the sick; the Lord will raise
him up, and if he has committed any sins, he will be
forgiven (James 5:15).

Many times when people get sick and are admitted
to the hospital, they expect their pastors and church elders to just know by the Spirit to come anoint them with
oil and pray.

Now, once in a while, the Lord does deal with me
regarding an individual who is having physical problems.
When that happens, I'll usually either call that person
myself or have someone else call him to see how he is
doing.

However, sometimes the people I call will shut me off before I get the first few sentences out of my mouth. Why? Because they don't want to be honest with their pastor about their trials and their weaknesses. They may also feel ashamed that they have consulted a doctor about their condition, thinking that I'll judge them as weak in faith.

I want to emphasize this point: *Don't ever act condescending toward people who go to a doctor.* Without doctors, my friend, a great many Christians would be dead!

If I were in a life-or-death situation and people asked me, "What do you think you're going to do to get healed?" I'd just respond, "Anything I can!" I wouldn't try to be a superhero of faith who dogmatically refused to go to a doctor. I wouldn't want to risk causing people to go the rest of their lives not believing in divine healing because I did something stupid!

People in my congregation often have the idea, "Pastor Robb doesn't believe in doctors." I better believe in doctors, because many people in my church wouldn't live if they didn't go to the doctor! I'll tell you the real truth about the matter: I believe *beyond* doctors. I believe God's hand is upon people's lives to help them reach His goal of divine health and healing for their physical bodies.

So when you're sick, make sure you don't immediately run to the doctor for your solution. First run to God! But if you decide to go to a doctor, do so without feeling any sense of condemnation, guilt, or shame. Your faith is still intact; you can still believe God for your healing as you seek Him first.

Anointing the sick with oil is an avenue of healing that can certainly pertain to many types of situations, but it is most effective when the sick individual is young in the Lord and in need of forgiveness and freedom. When the church elders anoint the young believer with oil and pray for him, a reassurance of the Holy Spirit's Presence and healing power is imparted to his life.

Let the Holy Spirit Lead You

We've looked at six different avenues of healing presented in the Word of God. The seventh avenue will be the subject of the next chapter. So how do you know which avenue the Holy Spirit wants to use to effect a healing and a cure in your body? You have to seek the Lord as you pursue your healing. Ask Him what direction He would have you take in order to obtain the healing you desire.

You will usually sense a specific leading of the Holy Spirit as to which avenue of healing to take in a given situation. For instance, after seeking the Lord about the matter, you may know in your heart, *I'm supposed to go to church tonight and have hands laid on me to be healed.* Or you may sense a leading to deal with the issue in your own prayer closet.

But here's something I've discovered through my many years of ministry and walking with the Lord: The more you mature in the Lord, the more the Holy Spirit will lead you in the direction of the final avenue of healing we're going to discuss — *believing the Word for yourself.* Every other avenue actually works toward this goal. Jesus spoke of this principle in Luke 7:2-10, where He told the centurion that the person with the greatest kind of faith was the one who simply believed His Word.

It's the truth — God's highest and best way for you to receive healing is to believe Him for yourself through a personal relationship with Him and the Holy Spirit. So let's talk about how to do just that!

Chapter 4

Believing God for Yourself

In order for you to learn how to obtain healing for your body through your own faith, you must first grasp this fact: *God has granted you healing as a part of His covenant with you through His Son, Jesus Christ.*

However, as I said before, healing is probably one of the most elusive graces God has given you in this life. The only proof you have for your healing until it is manifested in your body is that which the Word of God says.

When people come forward to have hands laid on them for healing, I often ask them, "Well, now, what do you believe? Do you believe you're going to be healed when hands are laid upon you?"

Many times they answer, "Well, I hope so."

It is evident that the Word of God isn't enough proof for people who answer like that. In fact, many people live and die in the begging mode with God. They beg the Lord to heal them, saying, "Oh, please, God! I promise I'll make a deal with You if You'll just heal me."

These people think if they make some kind of deal with God, He'll come through for them because He's a "give-and-take" kind of fellow. No, He's only a "give" kind of fellow!

My friend, nothing could be further from the truth. That's why it's so important to understand that the only proof of your healing you'll ever have before you see the manifestation is the Word of God. And you have to get to the place where God's Word is all the proof you need!

You see, when healing comes, it isn't always instantaneous, and it doesn't always "sound a trumpet." If you're not actively standing on God's Word in faith, you may not even recognize what He is doing to work a healing in your body.

Consider this: How many times have you prayed for healing, only to have the symptoms just gradually go away until you forgot you even had them?

The last thing the devil wants you to realize is that you got healed. In fact, he likes to keep you so busy that you forget the symptoms were ever there. Why is that? Because if you knew for sure that God healed you, you'd tell everyone about it! The devil does *not* want the world to know who healed you because it would once more demonstrate the truth of the Cross — this time, in *your* life!

Our Covenant-Making God

Verses scattered throughout the Old Testament reveal that healing has always been a part of God's covenant with His people. In fact, in Exodus 15:26, God called Himself "the Lord who heals you." The Hebrew name is Jehovah Rapha — the Lord God, our Healer. Thus, His covenant with us includes healing for our minds and bodies.

In Isaiah 53, God actually gave a description of the One called the suffering Redeemer, as well as the work this Redeemer would accomplish:

> **Surely He has borne our griefs and carried our sorrows; yet we esteemed Him stricken, smitten by God, and afflicted.**
> **But He was wounded for our transgressions, He was bruised for our iniquities; the chastisement for our peace was upon Him, and by His stripes we are healed.**
> **Isaiah 53:4, 5**

The truth in that scripture gets more exciting the more I think about it! The problem is, most people don't think about it. They don't spend their time pursuing its reality in their own personal experience. They allow their lives to go a thousand miles an hour, forgetting what Jesus really came to do for them through His death, burial, and resurrection.

When we come over to the New Testament, God's covenant of healing still remains, but something has significantly changed. Under the Old Covenant, the Lord was the Healer of His people. However, healing came from the outside prior to the Cross.

You see, everything in the Old Testament pointed toward the Cross and the redemptive work Jesus would one day accomplish. For instance, Isaiah 53:5 says, *"... by His stripes we are healed."* In the New Testament, Peter quotes this verse a little differently: *"...by whose stripes you WERE healed."* One scripture is looking *toward* the Cross; one is looking *backward* at the Cross. One is a truth to come; one is the truth in this present day.

Under the New Covenant, healing no longer comes *from without*; it now comes *from within*. Jesus explained this change in covenant to His disciples right before His death, saying in effect, "I've got to go away, but I'm going to send another Comforter to live in you and be with you forever. He will be your Helper, your Teacher, and your Friend" (John 14:16,17,26).

**Recognize That You Need
The Holy Spirit's Help**

Romans 8:26 tells us more about this Friend who dwells within us and will never forsake us:

> **Likewise the Spirit also helps in our weak-
> nesses. For we do not know what we should
> pray for as we ought, but the Spirit Himself
> makes intercession for us with groanings which
> cannot be uttered.**
>
> **Romans 8:26**

The Holy Spirit helps us in our weaknesses. He helps us in the midst of stress and pain. He helps us when we don't know what to pray for as we ought.

That word "helps" in the Greek carries the meaning *struggles for and against.* So the Holy Spirit struggles on our behalf against those things that attempt to encroach on our relationship with Him. He is our Paraclete — our Comforter, Helper, Standby, Intercessor, Counselor, Teacher, and Friend. He is the One who has been called alongside to help us. He's there to help us in all of our lives, in all of our ways, in everything we face each and every day.

Jesus sent the Comforter to help you because you need help. Now, it may be quite a revelation to you to realize that you can't make it on your own. But one of the worst problems you can inflict upon yourself is to refuse to ever admit to others that you need help.

You need to follow blind Bartimaeus' example. Remember, when Bartimaeus heard Jesus was coming, the Bible says he began to cry out for help, saying, *"...Jesus, Son of David, have mercy on me!"* (Mark 10:47). Religion told him to shut up, but Bartimaeus cried out all the

more. You see, you can't stop a person when he knows
he needs Jesus!

That's certainly one thing *I* have come to realize. I
need the Holy Ghost to help me. I need Him every day.
I need Him all the time. I have to draw on His strength
every second of my life with every ounce of energy I
can muster.

Let the Holy Spirit
Give Life to Your Body

Now, with that in mind, look at Romans 8:11: *"But if
the Spirit of Him who raised Jesus from the dead dwells
in you, He who raised Christ from the dead will also
give life to your mortal bodies through His Spirit who
dwells in you."* Remember, we're not talking about God
ministering to mankind from the outside any longer. We
are under the New Covenant, purchased by the blood of
Jesus. The Spirit of Almighty God now dwells in us to
give life to our mortal bodies!

The problem with many believers is that they don't
expect the Holy Spirit to do anything for them; therefore, they don't cry out to Him when sickness or disease
attacks their bodies and they need His help. Instead, fear
grips their minds and hearts and paralyzes them from
pursuing the healing that is rightfully theirs in Christ.

When you recognize that the only One who can help
you is the Holy Spirit, you put yourself in a position to
win against those physical symptoms. The Bible says
He will *give life* to your mortal body. Another transla-

tion adds that He will even *give new strength and vitality*.

The Holy Spirit will give new strength and vitality to you from the inside out. When your body feels weak, He'll make it strong. So stay continually aware of the Holy Spirit's Presence within. He lives inside you, ready to cause new life and strength to spring up within you all the time. He's always ready to fulfill your every need and to be your Comforter in every situation.

But unless you acknowledge the Holy Spirit, He cannot do that for you. Proverbs 3:6 says, *"In all your ways acknowledge Him, and He shall direct your paths."* In *all* your ways, you are to acknowledge Him. That's how you open the door to His help, guidance, and strength.

Unfortunately, people often apply that scripture to their lives backwards. They figure out what they want to do with their lives and then start telling everyone, "This is what the Lord told me." When they do that, they're destroying their own lives and trying to get you to sanction something you know is not of the Lord!

Don't make that same mistake. Make sure you acknowledge the leadership of the Holy Spirit in every area of your life, including your pursuit of healing. He will give strength and vitality to your body and direct your path each step of the way until you receive the desire of your heart — a life of divine health!

Draw On
The Holy Spirit's Strength

Perhaps you've been feeling physically tired and run-down lately. Let me tell you a sure-fire way to draw on the Holy Spirit's power to quicken your mortal body. Number one, spend your time thinking about Ephesians 6:10: *"Finally, my brethren, be strong in the Lord and in the power of His might."* As you continue to meditate on that scripture and confess it over your body, life, strength, and vitality will be imparted to your mortal body by the Spirit who lives in you.

My wife Linda and I know this works because we've see the power of Ephesians 6:10 operating in our own lives. In years gone by, we could make it on just a few hours' sleep each night as we continually depended on the Lord for strength. These days I seem to need a bit more sleep than I did then — at least three and a half hours. Otherwise, I feel just a bit disheveled!

Why don't more believers experience this quickening of their mortal bodies by the Holy Spirit? Because they read what is in the Book, but they never allow what is in the Book to permeate their lives. That doesn't make any more sense than a person who goes to Denny's just to look at the menu. He loves to stare at those delicious-looking pictures, but he never tastes the food!

Replace Your Thoughts
With God's Thoughts

The next thing you should do to draw on the Holy Spirit's strength is take some time to rest your mind. You may need to go to sleep a little bit earlier. Most importantly, you should practice replacing your negative thoughts with God's life-giving thoughts, found in His Word.

You see, depression is just a series of unchecked negative thoughts. It's a result of one destructive thought after another bombarding your mind without you saying to those thoughts, *"No, no, no, no!* You're not coming here!"

Have you ever had a stray dog hang around your porch? Well, just because he hangs around your porch doesn't mean you have to let him in your living room. And just because Satan tries to insert negative thoughts into your mind, that doesn't mean you have to let those thoughts in and then continually dwell on them!

To practice thought replacement, you have to begin to rid your mind of all the negative things that happened in the past or that might happen in the future. For instance, if you start thinking, *I don't like myself*, get rid of that thought by replacing it with Ephesians 5:29: *"For no one ever hated his own flesh, but nourishes and cherishes it, just as the Lord does the church.*

Or you may be thinking, *I feel tired and weak.* Replace that thought with Isaiah 40:31: *"But those who wait on the Lord shall renew their strength; they shall mount up with wings like eagles, they shall run and not be weary, they shall walk and not faint.* " That word "renew" can also be translated "exchange." As you wait upon the Lord on a daily basis, you begin to exchange your strength for His strength.

Now, it's important to understand this: To wait upon God doesn't mean you're like a person sitting at a bus stop, passively waiting for the next bus to come. It means you are poised to respond to the next instruction you receive from Him.

When I wait on God, I don't have anyone else in the room with me. No one else sits at the table. I do everything I can to make His wish my command, His thoughts my thoughts. Because I do this, I exchange my strength for His and thus mount up with wings as an eagle. I run. I do not get weary. I walk and I do not faint!

I know from firsthand experience how much power there is in faithfully practicing this divine exchange. You see, I got saved in a mental institution in 1975. I originally was admitted there because of a condition diagnosed as ambiguous anxiety. Later the doctors changed the diagnosis to a deep character disorder. They helped me through the toughest part but then told me there was nothing more they could do for me; I was going to be that way for the rest of my life.

But then I got born again! God absolutely delivered me overnight from a mental disorder that was supposedly incurable. When it was time for me to be released, the doctors said they would see me soon. Nine out of ten people who were ever released from that mental institution ended up coming back. But I made the decision in my heart that I would *not* be back. If nine out of ten people returned, I determined that I would be number ten!

I spent the next few years being a nice but ignorant Christian boy. I didn't know how to *keep* my victory in the mental realm. I didn't know I was supposed to exchange my thoughts for God's thoughts, and Satan was taking advantage of my ignorance.

Then I learned that by failing to exchange my thoughts for God's thoughts, my mind had been open game for Satan's strategies. I realized I couldn't control who might knock at the door of my mind, but I *could* determine whom I let in!

I began to live by this simple rule: If God speaks something, I choose to let that in my mind. If God isn't the one who spoke it, it is *not* coming in. I can attribute one hundred percent of the deliverance I've enjoyed over the years to practicing this one basic rule!

Build a New Foundation
According to 'Heavenly Genetics'

Jesus prayed for us in John 17:17 (KJV), saying, *"Sanctify them through thy truth: thy word is truth."* That means we are actually set apart by the truth, which, according to Jesus, is the Word of God.

That mental institution was *a* truth. Those heart symptoms were *a* truth. The flu is *a* truth. Diabetes is *a* truth. Arthritis is *a* truth. But the Word of God is *the* truth!

We are not to deny the symptoms that attack our bodies. Many people who think they are in faith are actually in denial. That isn't what we are doing. The sickness is there, and it is real. But it is only "*a*" truth.

"A truth" may affect your life because of your determinisms, such as your genetic disposition or your learned thought patterns. The world will tell you a number of reasons why this "truth" is occurring in your life.

For instance, people will give you several natural reasons why you are sick or why you aren't enjoying the good health you desire. Often they want to know if any of your family members ever suffered from a similar condition. They also want to know about every other physical condition or disease that has occurred within your family. You'll find these types of questions on insurance forms, employment forms, government forms, etc. These questions pertain to your *genetic imprint*.

The genetic imprint is a method to identify who you are in certain natural aspects. If a doctor can learn about your genetic imprint, he can tell you whether or not you have a propensity toward cancer, diabetes, and so forth, long before the disease ever attacks. If you are genetically set up to contract a particular disease, a doctor may tell you that such a prospect is likely.

Insurance companies want to obtain your genetic imprint for their own purposes. With this information, they determine whether or not you are insurable and, if so, what kind of insurance you will be able to get. It is all a money game to them, and it all ties into your natural genetic imprint.

That's why it's so important to live life from a foundational perspective. By that, I mean *you must begin to build your life on a solid foundation of God's Word rather than on the world's opinions and standards of judgment.*

First, you have to dig out of your life all those natural determinisms that hinder your success in God. In Luke 6:47,48, Jesus said, *"Whoever comes to Me, and hears My sayings and does them, I will show you whom he is like: He is like a man building a house, WHO DUG DEEP AND LAID THE FOUNDATION on the rock...."*

I started digging deep before I laid a spiritual foundation in my life. I dug out the fact that my mother was an alcoholic. I dug out the fact that my dad had a heart attack when he was a young man and then died of cancer. I knew I had to dig out all those genetic determinisms that Satan wanted to use to defeat me. Then I had to begin to replace those natural obstacles with the truth of the Word.

My earthly father may have had genetic deficiencies, but my Heavenly Father has given to me something different. No matter what my genetic imprint looks like, by the stripes of Jesus I am healed!

Your favorite auntie may have gotten sick with a terminal disease when she was thirty years old, but that doesn't mean you have to be just like her. You can live the life of divine health God intended for you!

So go through the foundation of your life. Dig out all your negative memories, all your harmful relationships, and all the deficiencies of your own genetic imprint. Then lay a solid foundation according to the Word of God (Matt. 7:24-27; 1 Cor. 3:11).

As for me, I tell the Lord, "Father, my genealogy only goes back to the day I got saved. My history starts October 28, 1975. I don't care about who I was or what I was like before that day. It doesn't matter to me. I am no longer European in descent; I am now "Heavenian." I am a citizen of Heaven, not a citizen of this earth!"

You see, when we come to Jesus, we are "re-fathered." Titus 3:5 says we have been saved *"not by works of righteousness which we have done, but according to His mercy He saved us, through THE WASHING OF RE-GENERATION and renewing of the Holy Spirit."*

One meaning of the word "regeneration" is *re-engineered*. I received new genetics at the time I received Jesus. God gave me heavenly genetics! I now look like God on the inside of me. My spirit man shares the same description attributed to Jesus in Hebrews 1:3: *"Who being the brightness of His glory and the express image of His person...."*

I am a perfect imprint of who God is because of what Jesus did for me. I don't live life according to the external world any longer. I am not the sick trying to get healed. I am the healed, and someone is trying to steal my health. I am not the depressed trying to be free from fear. I am the courageous, and someone is trying to steal my courage. That is the perspective I live by as I exchange my natural thoughts for God's thoughts of life and freedom.

This is the higher realm you begin to walk in as you practice thought replacement. You are renewing your mind with God's Word, which is the first step to discovering and fulfilling the good, acceptable, and perfect will of God for your life: *"And do not be conformed to this world, but be transformed by the renewing of your mind, that you may prove what is that good and acceptable and perfect will of God"* (Rom. 12:2). It is also the first step to believing God for your own healing!

Meditate on the Word

A key factor in replacing your carnal thoughts with God's thoughts is *meditation on and confession of God's Word.* God talked about this principle in Joshua 1:8: *"This Book of the Law shall not depart from your mouth, but you shall meditate in it day and night, that you may observe to do according to all that is written in it. For then you will make your way prosperous, and then you will have good success."*

When you meditate on the Word day and night, you begin to see pictures of yourself doing all that is written therein. You have no time to see yourself differently than God sees you if you're meditating on His Word day and night. This is how you make your way prosperous. This is how you enjoy good success!

You may remember that the word "prosperous" is also used in Third John 2, where it says, *"Beloved, my greatest desire above all is that you would prosper and be in health even as your soul prospers."* In order for a person's body to be well, his soul must prosper. But his soul will only prosper when he accesses the information he needs. That information is found in God's Word, and it provides spiritual food for spiritual strength, just as a person's physical body needs natural food for physical strength.

As you draw on your relationship with the Holy Spirit by meditating on God's Word, the Holy Spirit begins to paint His picture of who you already are inside of you. You begin to realize, "This is who I *am*, not *who I am going to be*. I don't need to go looking on the outside for my healing. I don't need to have hands laid on me. I don't need the working of miracles to operate on my behalf. God may lead me to pursue one of these other avenues of healing in a particular situation. But I believe that by the stripes of Jesus, I *was* healed. If I *was* healed, then I *am* healed, so it's time to get myself out of bed and begin to behave like a healed person!"

I remember a time years ago when a fellow coworker would come to my home every weekday morning and I'd disciple him before we went off to work. One morning, this man witnessed firsthand a demonstration of what I had been teaching him about faith and healing.

I just wasn't doing well physically that day. Everything in my body said I was going to die. Actually, we lived on the second floor, and I didn't think I could even take a step to get downstairs to my car.

I went to God and said, "Father, I don't understand what's happening here."

Then the Lord spoke to my heart: "Tell Me — what have you been meditating on? What have you been thinking about?"

I said, "Father, I've been thinking and meditating on the fact that by the stripes of Jesus, I was healed. By the stripes of Jesus, I am well."

"Then get up," the Lord said. "If that's what you've been meditating on, get up! Healed men go to work!"

I got on my feet and took my first step. Immediately strength came back into my body! By the time I made it down to my car, I was feeling so good, I started dancing around it!

Luke 17:14 tells us that as the lepers went to the priests in obedience to Jesus' instruction, they were cleansed. In the same way, as you get up and act healed in obedience to the Holy Spirit's leading, you will be healed. Many times, people want to wait until they feel better before they act healed. They say, "As soon as I get healed, I'll get up and take care of that."

If that's what you're saying, you will never get it. It is *as you go* — as you act in faith like you already have your answer — that you will receive your healing.

Years ago when I worked as a package car driver for United Parcel Service, I had to deliver packages to a large aluminum company. Every one of the packages I delivered to this company was always at the upper limit of the maximum weight allowed. Well, I didn't have a very good back. It seemed as if I could cause my back to go out just by looking at someone the wrong way! And if I leaned the wrong way over a counter to plug something into the wall, I could be flat on my back for three days.

One day I was delivering packages to this aluminum company, and my back was giving me fits. Every time I went to try to lift something up, the pain was horrible. It was so excruciating at times that I'd dropped the package I was holding.

My body was screaming, "Just cash it in! Give it up. Forget it. You can't make it. There is too much pain!"

I did have a tremendous amount of pain. But instead of giving in to it, I spoke out the words I had been meditating on through this whole ordeal with my back: "No, by the stripes of Jesus, I am healed! I am not going to *get* healed; I *am* healed. I am not waiting to get well; I *am* well. And if I am healed, then I'm going to deliver this stuff!"

To some who have heard this testimony, what happened next was unbelievable. I was immediately healed right there on the spot! Since that day more than fifteen years ago, I have never had any more trouble with my back. The Holy Spirit gave life to my mortal body as a result of my meditation on God's Word!

So begin to find the scriptures that correspond with every area of your life. How are you supposed to feel about your brother in Christ? How do you forgive? When do you forgive? How do you become prosperous? How do you get healthy? What about your self-esteem? How are you to feel about yourself? Let your Heavenly Father dictate how you feel and what you think. Don't allow your carnal feelings to dictate how your life will be.

God answers every subject of an individual's life *"...precept upon precept, line upon line, line upon line, here a little, there a little"* (Isa. 28:10). That's why we must follow His instructions in Proverbs 4:20-22:

My son, give attention to my words; incline your ear to my sayings.
Do not let them depart from your eyes; keep them in the midst of your heart;
For they are life to those who find them, and health to all their flesh.

When I was first learning how to meditate on the Word, I'd sometimes put a scripture card on my car windshield in my line of vision. After all, the Bible says, *"Do not let them depart from your eyes..."*! Every time I'd take my eyes off that scripture card, my mind would begin to think crazy thoughts again. So I'd pull my eyes back to read the scripture again and again. After practicing this for a while, the scriptures I kept before my eyes eventually became more real to me than those old, carnal thoughts. Little by little, my life began to conform to the Word I was meditating on rather than to the circumstances I was living in!

Be a Doer and Not Just a Hearer
Of the Word

God also tells us to *"...keep them* [God's words] *in the midst of your heart."* One of the biggest problems Christians have is the fact that they don't keep the Word of God in the midst of their heart. James warns believers not to make that mistake when he says, *"But be doers of the word, and not hearers only, deceiving yourselves"* (James 1:22).

Some individuals have heard the Word a great deal but never seem to be able to get it. Instead, they focus on their physical condition. They like to tell anyone who will listen all about it. However, these people don't get five feet ahead of where they are right now in their spiritual walk!

That's the reason the Body of Christ has such a problem. So many people are being preached to, and so few are actually doers of the Word!

Most churches hold "Christian nursery" every week with long-time Christians instead of making room for the new babes in Christ who are getting saved. The "older kids" should be taking care of the "younger kids" in church. Certainly that's the way it is in most natural families. But instead, the "older kids" get offended because they think the pastor isn't properly taking care of them. They complain, "The pastor isn't spending time with me. He's not calling me to see how I'm doing."

But the pastor is supposed to concentrate on taking care of those in the congregation who are young in the

Lord. The older Christians should be helping these new Christians grow up in the Lord, but too many of them keep hearing the Word without actually doing it.

God said, "If you will not only *hear* but also *do* the Word, you will be blessed in your deeds" (James 1:25). That's how to build a solid foundation on the Word so you can believe God for your own healing!

Chapter 5

Adjusting Your 'Receiver'

The Holy Ghost lives on the inside of you, my friend, to perform whatever it is you need. Every day, He's on the inside of you to bring your body closer to absolute, perfect health — and He does it through First Peter 2:24: *"Who Himself bore our sins in His own body on the tree, that we, having died to sins, might live for righteousness — by whose stripes you were healed."*

Now, why did God tell us this? Because so many believers live with guilt and shame, always plagued with thoughts of the sins they've committed or the good things they haven't done, always feeling unworthy to receive God's blessings.

The sad truth is that far too many patients in this nation's mental institutions are Christians. How did many of them get there? They spent their lives always feeling guilty. They continually thought about past sins and how much they had missed it. They felt like God and others were always judging them because they could have done so much better in life.

Let me tell you something about your life, my friend. The best you'll ever be in life is a number six. You'll never be a perfect number seven, no matter how hard you try. As a matter of fact, the more perfect you want to live, the more frustrated you'll be. The more perfect you try to be, the more imperfections you will reveal about yourself. The sooner you accept that fact, the easier it will be to receive God's healing mercies, as well as every other blessing He wants to give you.

The Problem Is in the 'Receiver'

I'll tell you something else that will help you if you'll take it to heart: When it comes to divine healing, the main issue isn't *what you know*; it's *what you are able to receive*.

If you turned on your car radio and heard no sound, no matter how much you turned your tuning dial, you probably wouldn't think, *I can't believe none of those radio stations are working today!* No, you'd realize that the problem wasn't in all the different transmitters; the problem was in *the receiver*.

You need to have as much common sense when it comes to your healing. If you've had difficulty receiving the healing you know is a part of your spiritual inheritance in Christ, maybe you need to adjust your "receiver"!

Consider the Old Testament account of Naaman and the prophet Elisha. Naaman is an example of someone who had to fix his receiver before God could heal his body.

Naaman was a captain in the Syrian army who had recently led Syria to a great victory in battle. Although he was known as "a mighty man of valor," Naaman was also a leper (2 Kings 5:1).

Then a young Jewish maidservant of Naaman's wife told her mistress, *"...If only my master were with the prophet who is in Samaria! For he would heal him of his leprosy"* (2 Kings 5:3).

So Naaman went to the king of Syria and told him what the Jewish maidservant had said. The king responded in effect, "I'll write the king of Israel, and we'll get this all straightened out. Go saddle up the camels, pal. And take ten talents of silver and six thousand shekels of gold along with you!" (vv. 4,5).

To make a long story short, Naaman traveled to Israel and knocked on the prophet Elisha's front door. But the man of God didn't come to the door himself. Instead, he sent his servant to give Naaman instructions on how to receive his healing. And Naaman got offended! You see, Naaman had a problem with his receiver.

Gehazi the servant gave the prophet's simple instructions to Naaman: "Go wash yourself in the Jordan. Dip yourself seven times, and you'll be clean of your leprosy." That ticked Naaman off! The Bible says, *"...he turned and went away in a rage"* (v. 12).

Finally, Naaman's servants came to him and said, "Now, wait a second, Master. If the prophet had told you to do something difficult, you would have done it. Why not just do what he's instructed you to do?" (v. 13).

So Naaman finally listened to his servants and adjusted his "receiver." After obeying Elisha's simple instructions to dip seven times in the Jordan River, Naaman walked out of that river completely cleansed of his leprosy!

Different Kinds of Reception Problems

Have you ever had a response similar to Naaman's when you found out what God said in His Word about a particular problem you were facing? "You mean, it's that easy? That's all it takes? Now, wait a minute. Give me something hard to do. You know, let me eat shards of glass; let me crawl naked on thumbtacks. Give me something hard so I can prove I deserve God's blessings!"

This is the problem with many people's "receivers." They have the misconception that difficulty is where God lives. But that isn't true. God already knows that in the scope of eternity, you and I don't have our act together yet. He takes that fact into account when He asks us to do something. He *wants* us to receive His blessings, so His instructions are simple and clear: We are to obey the leading of His Spirit within and walk according to His Word.

Other believers develop a problem with their receivers when they start comparing their own level of faith for healing with other people's faith level. If their faith seems stronger, these same people conclude that they have their act together and can therefore receive their healing all on their own according to their own terms.

But these people are only deceiving themselves. Everyone in the Body of Christ has a different area of strength. Some have an easier time believing for money or relationships; others can more easily believe for healing.

The point is, we all need each other. The devil likes to get us to a place where we isolate ourselves and thus develop a problem with reception. But we need the encouragement of other believers to help us receive the healing God wants to give us. Our words of encouragement or doubt greatly affect not only our own ability to receive, but also that of fellow believers.

Think about it: What if the only thing a person with a terminal illness heard from other Christians was "Man, no one has ever been healed of that before"? That person would probably die! But imagine what it would be like if that same person only heard words of encouragement: "You can do this! You can receive your healing. You can get it!" Do you know what would happen? That person's faith would be strengthened and energized to receive his supernatural healing!

I'll tell you another problem many Christians have that affects their ability to receive God's blessings: They take the things of God for granted. They just want to sit in a pew and never really do much to help their local church or further the Kingdom of God. They're the ones who often hear and hear the Word but never really act on it. They are also the ones who don't usually receive their healing!

Another reason so many believers stay sick is that they are critical of any teaching on faith and divine healing. Why? Well, people often criticize what they don't understand. They are ignorant of all that Jesus purchased for them through His death on the Cross. Hosea 4:6 says, *"My people are destroyed for lack of knowledge...."*

Interestingly enough, many times the very people who criticize divine healing the most are the ones who work the hardest to get it. They're the ones who make sure they eat the right things and work out three times a week. They're the ones who make an appointment with the doctor when they *think* they're going to come down with the flu "because it's so hard to get into the doctor."

These people are like the fellow who said, "Four times in a row I have bought nonrefundable airline tickets for a family vacation, and each time someone got so sick, we couldn't go. You watch and see — as sure as shootin', as soon as I go buy airline tickets, someone is going to come up sick!" Then when someone does get sick, he says, "You see? I told you so!" That person's faith in someone getting sick made his own expectations a manifested reality! If only he could have used his faith to believe God for something he *couldn't* see!

So make sure you always listen to the teaching of the Word with a hungry heart, because God doesn't fill a critical spirit. And if you *have* been criticizing the things of God instead of embracing them, don't waste any time adjusting your receiver. Don't let a critical spirit block God's power from giving life, healing, and new strength to your mortal body!

Don't Listen to the Wrong People

Some well-meaning people who actually believe in prosperity and healing still spend their time wondering why healing hasn't come. They think they're doing right, yet they wonder why they're always dealing with one sickness or another.

These people experience defeat because they're making some of the same mistakes the children of Israel did in the wilderness. Number one, *they are listening to the wrong people.*

God had led the children of Israel out of Egypt and given them the Promised Land. He had told His people, "This land is yours. Every place on which your foot shall tread belongs to you."

Then God told Moses, "Tell twelve spies to go spy out at the land. Just tell them to take a look and afterwards come back and report to you" (Num. 13:2).

When the twelve spies returned from spying out the land, two men were carrying a huge cluster of grapes on a big branch. They said, "Surely that is a land flowing with milk and honey! And here is the fruit thereof!" (Num. 13:27). Those grapes were as big as golf balls!

Joshua and Caleb stood up and said, "Listen, we are well able to take the land. Let's go get it!"

But the other ten stood up and said, "We are *not* well able! We can't do it. The inhabitants are fierce. Things are rough. Not only that, but we saw the children of Anak — the giants. You should have seen how big those giants are! They're absolutely huge and *mean*! We can't go up and take that land!"

Then the ten spies made a profound statement: *"...We were like grasshoppers in our own sight, and so we were in their sight"* (Num. 13:33). Isn't it interesting that you become in the sight of others what you are in your own sight?

The children of Israel heard both reports but decided to listen to the wrong people. And as a result of accepting the ten spies' evil report of doubt and unbelief, the older generation of Israelites was unable to receive and enjoy their Promised Land of blessing and abundance.

On the other hand, God rewarded Joshua and Caleb for their faith by eventually allowing them to enter the Promised Land. However, the two faithful men first had to put up with forty more years in the wilderness with a bunch of unbelieving people!

Watch Who You Associate With

This brings up the second mistake Christians make that hinders them from receiving healing for their bodies, even though they may believe in divine healing. This important principle directly affects one's ability to receive from God: *Be careful in choosing the people you spend time with.*

If you're not careful, you might spend the next forty-five years of your life paying the price for what some unbelieving person did. You could miss out on the best God has for your life just because you wanted to hang around with the wrong people!

You pay the price for the people you are with. Your life is largely what it is today because of the relationships you've made in every arena of life — friends, family members, coworkers, fellow church members, etc. Every relationship you have either takes you up or takes you down.

So even though Joshua and Caleb believed God's promises, they still had to wander in the wilderness with the rest of the Israelites for the next forty years. Think about that: The children of Israel walked around in circles within an area of twenty-five square miles for forty years! Do you know what they were doing? They were coming to a place where they finally believed God — and Joshua and Caleb had to go along for the ride!

Word Preached
Not Mixed With Faith

Another mistake the children of Israel made that Christians make as well is described in Hebrews 4:2: *"For indeed the gospel was preached to us as well as to them; but the word which they heard did not profit them, NOT BEING MIXED WITH FAITH IN THOSE WHO HEARD IT."*

Now look at Hebrews 4:1,2 as translated in the *Message Bible*:

For as long, then, as that promise of resting in him pulls us on to God's goal for us, we need to be careful that we're not disqualified. We received the same promises as those people in the wilderness, but THE PROMISES DIDN'T DO THEM A BIT OF GOOD BECAUSE THEY DIDN'T RECEIVE THE PROMISES WITH FAITH.

Everything was right there for the children of Israel. The Promised Land was theirs to possess. But they didn't receive that promise with faith and therefore missed out on enjoying its fulfillment.

As the Israelites wandered for those forty years in the wilderness, they probably blamed God for the fact that they were going to die without ever entering the Promised Land. But it wasn't God's fault they never received what He had given them. They never mixed the promise they had heard with faith. And in the end, they received none of it.

That is the same mistake many Christians make today. Their desire for knowledge has accelerated, but they have unhooked from what the Holy Spirit wants them to do with that knowledge! They often end up congregating in little "prayer groups," where they spend hours upon hours discussing exegetical tidbits of information that will not change their lives whatsoever. They may have a relationship with something they learned *about* God, but they know nothing about developing a personal relationship *with* God.

Often these Christians have heard a lot of Word. They've heard about divine healing and about how God wants them well. However, they haven't mixed faith with what they've heard. They know far more than they have ever lived.

These Christians just keep walking around the desert for thirty-nine years, taking a trip around the same mountain again and again. They say, "Well, I've seen this happen before. Every time I get excited for Jesus, the flu hits me. And the more I preach about healing, sickness attacks my body. I guess it will happen again this time!" And it usually does!

So when it comes time for these believers to receive healing, they miss out on what belongs to them in Christ because their receiver has a fundamental deficiency — a distinct lack of active faith.

The Importance of Your Foundation

That's why it's so important for you to live life from a foundational perspective. Nothing will help you improve your ability to receive from God more than building a solid foundation of His Word in your life.

When building a good foundation, everything boils down to this one question: "What does God say about this in His Word?"

You may feel tempted to say, "You know, I'm tired of hearing what God says about it. Why can't you just tell me a story or give me a 'how-to' book to read?"

I'll tell you why, my friend — because Jesus said, "Deal with your foundation." You don't have to build the "house" — in other words, perform the miracle you need. Jesus will do that. But He does expect you to build a good foundation.

How many people come over to your house and say, "Man, you have an awesome-looking foundation"? No one ever does! But people do come over and say, "Gosh, you have a nice house!"

Nevertheless, your house is nothing without the foundation. How would you like your friends to come over and see your house with a big crack right down the middle? They'd say, "Wow! What happened to your nice house?" The problem wasn't the house. The problem was the poor foundation.

Jesus expresses God's heart on this subject in Luke 6:46-49 (*Message*):

> **"Why are you so polite with me, always saying 'Yes, sir,' and 'That's right, sir,' but never doing a thing I tell you? These words I speak to you are not mere additions to your life, homeowner improvements to your standard of living. They are foundation words, words to build a life on.**
>
> **"If you work the words into your life, you are like a smart carpenter who dug deep and**

laid the foundation of his house on bedrock. When the river burst its banks and crashed against the house, nothing could shake it; it was built to last. But if you just use my words in Bible studies and don't work them into your life, you are like a dumb carpenter who built a house but skipped the foundation. When the swollen river came crashing in, it collapsed like a house of cards. It was a total loss."

Every area of your life — whether it's marriage, children, finances, job, or healing — has a list of foundational principles to be followed in order to achieve success. Every one of those basic principles are found in God's Word. Thus, adjusting your receiver can be as simple as acting on the Word you have heard in any given area.

You see, there is a requirement for everything in life, my friend. Salvation is free, but experiencing God's abundant life — which includes divine healing — costs you something. *You have to build your foundation solidly on God's Word!*

This is especially true in the area of healing. It isn't necessarily what you believe at the time you get sick that's important. What *is* important is how much time you put into building your foundation before sickness ever shows up!

Choose To Press In

As I told you earlier, God has given me a mandate to bring you deeper into your relationship with God so you can walk in abundance and divine health. But you must *choose to press in.* You must choose to go deeper. You have to stir up your hunger for things of God. Cry out for Him day and night. Look for His guidance in every situation.

As you pursue God's healing promises for your own life, remember this: There is always a payback day with Him. You see, God is an Investor. He doesn't invest in His children without expecting a return. And He doesn't request obedience from His children without *giving* a return!

Remember the parable of the steward who just hid the one talent he was given until his master came back (Matt. 25:14-30)? His master called him a "wicked servant"! Then the master said, "Throw this man out. Take him to the outer darkness where there is weeping and gnashing of teeth. Get rid of him!"

On the other hand, the steward who said, "Look, Master. I had five talents, and I've made five more" received a commendation from his master. The master said, "Well done, good and faithful servant! Enter into the joy of the Lord." It was payback day for that servant!

Expect *your* payback day to come, too, as you diligently build a solid foundation of the Word in your life. You'll watch as man's opinions and faulty religious doctrines about healing lose all significance to you. Meanwhile, the healing promises of God will become a vital, living reality in your heart.

Just trust the Holy Spirit within and God's anointed Word to guide you on the avenue of healing you should take. As long as you pursue healing God's way, you're headed straight for your desired destination of healing, wholeness, and a life of divine health!

For Further Information

For additional copies of this book,
for further information
regarding Robb Thompson's ministry schedule,
or for a complete listing of Robb Thompson's
books, audiotapes, and videotapes,
please write or call:

Family Harvest Church
18500 92nd Ave.
Tinley Park, IL 60477
1-877-WIN-LIFE
(1-877-946-5433)